Africa

Munu's
new home

Munu was feeling very happy as he munched on the spiky leaves of a magical euphorbia tree,
the sticky sap was delicious to hungry rhinos! 'Yum-yum,' said Munu, his rubbery lips pulling on his favourite tree.
The branch tickled his nose as he sucked and chewed.

Polly the oxpecker squawked loudly as she landed on Munu's flat horn. 'I saw everything,' she boasted.
Polly followed Munu everywhere, she liked the small bugs that landed on him and he was a very special friend.

Munu was feeling very important after his big adventure and now that he knew that he was 'a very special rhino'.

Dada the hadada landed on the post of Munu's boma, 'hadada!' he screeched.
He too had flown high in the sky and followed Munu. In the distance Munu could hear
Rumbelow and Zina, his new friendly rhino neighbours, trundling towards him.

Jafari, the gangly giraffe, was on his way too. Softly padding along was Malek, the lion.
He had woken from his afternoon nap and was looking forward to a story before his evening meal.

A gentle breeze cooled the hot African sun as all the friends gathered.
They were keen to hear Munu's story, and he was very excited to tell them.

Just before Munu settled down to tell his tale to his new friends,
his lily-like ears heard a rustle in the dry grass.

Chike the grass snake was here.
He always enjoyed an adventure and was quick to spread any news.

Chike slithered next to Munu, his bright iridescent scales gleaming in the sun.
'Is it true you were rescued and are now famous, Munu?' he hissed.

As everyone gathered around, Munu felt himself blush with excitement. His face burned with pride and was the colour of the red African soil. *I hope no one notices*, he thought, but secretly he was very pleased with all the attention.

Munu took a deep breath, and then he began to tell them his story and why he was such a special rhino. His friends fell silent and their eyes became as large as saucers as they listened to his tale.

Munu told them that he had taken a walk deep into the African bush.

'I walked so far that I no longer knew where I was.'

'Be careful Munu' was the last message of his kindly mother, Zemora, that rung in his ears.

Munu lived in the Bushveld in the heart of South Africa, the home of the San people and the land of the elephant, rhino and springbok, and of the monkeys that chatter and play all day.

There were so many things to see and do but, there were dangers too and every young rhino had to be very careful.

Munu continued, 'the sun was low and I walked into the path of an enormous male rhino. It was Zuma the Great (and grumpy), known across the land. His ears were large and his horn so big and shiny that it glinted in the setting sun.'

Zuma had a big craggy behind that looked like the surface of the moon and his body was the colour of earth.

Rhinos have roamed this land for millions of years. 'We are pre-historic and almost as old as the dinosaurs,' said Munu proudly.

Zuma was a grand old age and respected by all the young rhinos even though he could be a little bit grumpy at times!

Munu marvelled at his incredible stories of poachers who stole the horns from rhinos and sold them as trinkets to faraway lands. These poachers were bad people who hurt and injured rhinos.

'Be careful young ones and watch your step,' Zuma would say. He was very wise, and he cared for all his rhino kind. He had seen many wild animals disappear this way and that made him very sad.

Zuma stared at Munu and met his fuzzy gaze, 'hello Munu,' he grunted, 'there is a big storm coming from the West. I can hear the wind now making its journey towards us.'

'Hello Zuma,' said Munu, impressed that he was talking to the great rhino. The law of the land was that no young rhino should walk or talk in the shadow of their elders. Zuma raised his great grey horn like a weather vane high in the air and sniffed, 'yes it's coming Munu.'

The ground rumbled as Zuma then moved on, 'be careful Munu,' he called, as his deep voice faded and the wind picked up and arrived like a great event across the African plains.

Munu told his friends how the Kalahari wind had rustled and moved at great speed, and how small acacia trees turned to tumbleweed, rolling and spinning.

He told them how the wind was laughing and whistling and shaking the sandy earth so that it wrapped everything in its path.

'I was surrounded by a blanket of swirling pink and yellow sand and spun round and round, like a spider weaving a fly in its web,' he told them.

Munu was in the 'eye' of the storm. No longer was the sun bright or the land full of small green trees. It was dark, and Munu was scared.

Munu roamed in a circle, round and round.

He could not see, so he could not tell in which direction he was heading.

Round and round he went as the night drew in and the wind waved goodbye.
The noise from the African bush was still but for the chirruping of the crickets
and the chattering of the fruit bats. The fireflies hung like fairy lights in the dark night
but he could not see them.

The man in the moon watched over him and the stars twinkled. 'Don't worry Munu,' they
chimed, 'rest and get some sleep for tomorrow is another day.'

In the morning Munu had woken to the familiar squawk of Polly, who had been searching for her friend all night. 'Are you alright Munu?' she asked, as she ruffled her feathers and nestled into her favourite spot between his ears. Then another friendly voice. 'Is that you Munu?' said Brett, the wildlife ranger, 'that was quite a storm.'

Munu's head was hung low. He had not had a good night's sleep. 'Hello Polly, hello Brett,' Munu said, relieved that his friends had found him. Brett looked at Munu and saw he could no longer see. 'Don't worry,' he said, 'I'll take care of you Munu. We need to get a vet to look at your eyes.'

Munu waited patiently while Brett got a vet, and together they checked his eyes. Polly stayed close by, but she did not want to get in the way.

'Munu has lost his sight,' said the kindly vet. 'Oh dear,' said Brett, 'will Munu be okay?'
'Yes, Munu will be fine but now he will have to rely on his other super powers,' came the reply.

'He will use his nose to smell the flowers and shrubs, his tongue to taste the juicy leaves, his ears to hear the sounds of other animals and birds, and his voice to speak. Munu will do very well indeed.'

'Munu needs to go to a safe place where we can look after him,' said Brett.
'Munu is a very special rhino, he is a very rare black rhino. There are few of his kind left in Africa.
If we don't try to save these rare and incredible animals they will become extinct
and rhinos like Munu will be no more!'

'Am I special and rare?' Munu asked Polly.
'Yes, you are,' squawked Polly – she was very proud of her friend.

Munu told his friends that he was taken to a safe place where Brett, the vet and a small team of wildlife rangers took care of him. To ensure Munu was safe, they made his horn smaller so that it would not be trapped or damaged during his journey: it gave Munu a very special appearance.

Everyone was excited as a grand plan came together to move Munu to a sanctuary, a new home...a special place for Munu, where he would be safe and looked after. There were lots of happy animals there.

In no time at all, a rather large truck arrived. A banner flew gaily across it,

'Munu on the move' it said.

Brett was there with all the team.

'Steady away Munu,' said Brett, as the crate doors opened. Munu walked to get more of those juicy, delicious and magical leaves.

A jolt and a tug and Munu was in the air as his large crate was lifted from the ground.

Am I flying like Polly? thought Munu, as he rocked in his box from side to side.

A second jolt, and then a clunk, as the crate rested on the truck. 'Are you alright old boy?' said Brett. Munu made a loud mooing sound. Munu was fine and was on the move.

The wheels bounced as the truck and the team made their way to Munu's new home. It was very exciting!

Brett peered inside the crate, 'hello Munu,' he said with a smiley face, 'lots of people have come to welcome you to your new home.'

As Munu made his first careful steps out of the crate, he could hear everyone's delight.

A group of children were happy and singing, 'Hurrah – well done Munu!' they chorused.

Munu could tell there were lots of people and he felt very important. 'Hello everyone,' said Munu rather shyly, 'thank you for coming.'

'You've made the news Munu,' said Brett. 'You are a very special rhino.'

Munu cautiously trundled in to his new home, helped along by Polly, who found herself back on Munu's head. Polly was very excited, and a little flustered to have her moment in the spotlight too.

Munu could smell the freshly cut grass and hear the crowd cheer. 'There's lots for you to explore,' said Brett, 'and plenty of fresh euphorbia leaves and spiky noors, another delicious treat.'

This was a very special new home, thought Munu.

All the friends squawked, hissed, roared and screeched at their friend's adventure.

Chike the snake slithered with excitement and Dada sang 'hadada' in a very high pitch. Malek the lion let out a low roar of approval. Jafari the giraffe raised his long neck so high it looked like he would bump into the clouds and guffawed loudly. Rumbelow and Zina the rhinos, were ever so pleased to have a celebrity neighbour next door, and jostled side by side with happiness, as all the friends expressed their delight.

Brett returned, 'you're a star Munu,' he said clutching the local papers, 'and on the television too,' he said.

So Munu's big adventure had made headlines around the world
and Munu's face (with Polly too) was on the front page.

Munu may not be able to see, but now he is safe and he has so many things he can do. Munu was feeling very pleased and now it was time for his favourite pastime, a wallow in his new mud bath.

Polly made one loud squawk and flew to a nearby tree. She smiled down as Munu's large bottom slowly rolled over in the muddy water and made a loud squelching sound. *Mmmm*, thought Munu, as the big round bubbles covered the surface.

The magical euphorbia tree grew big and strong and so did Munu. In a world with people like Brett and children like you, many more Munus will thrive and survive.

The story of Munu and his friends hasn't ended, it's just beginning...

Munu and The White Lion Foundation

Recently The White Lion Foundation (TWLF) launched a major appeal to offer sanctuary and lifetime care to one of the world's rarest black rhinoceros, named Munu.

Munu was tragically blinded in territorial fighting and could no longer survive in the wild. He was discovered walking in circles on a South African reserve and was rescued by rangers. It was determined that there was no possibility of him regaining his sight.

The ambitious project to assist this 'special needs' rhino became the first major mission for TWLF. Through donations, Munu was able to be relocated to our specially prepared facility in the Eastern Cape. He now has full range on the new reserve. Here we can provide the safety, protection, and the additional care needed to allow him to thrive.

At the last official count there were only 254 south-western black rhinos left in South Africa – of which only perhaps 80 males are capable of breeding. Munu will be able to help father many more young rhinos and help contribute to the survival of his own species.

Munu requires full-time keepers and security at his new home at Founders Lodge by Mantis. Soon we hope to introduce him to a suitable female rhino, and any offspring will be donated to South Africa National Parks (SANparks) to further their conservation efforts of this endangered sub-species.

It is thanks to people like you buying this book and to others sending donations, that we will have the funds to help us establish a Rhino Rehabilitation Centre and Nursery for young orphaned calves in the Eastern Cape, together with our important relationship with SANParks and the success we have had with Munu, TWLF have been asked to urgently assist with other severely injured or orphaned rhinos in order to rehome, rehabilitate and eventually return them to the wild.

For more information or to donate to The White Lion Foundation, please visit our website: https://thewhitelion.foundation

The White Lion Foundation